Take Back Your Family Handbook

A 52-Week Game Plan to Create a Flourishing Family

Jefferson Bethke

NELSON BOOKS
An Imprint of Thomas Nelson

Take Back Your Family Handbook

Published in Nashville, Tennessee, by Nelson Books, an imprint of Thomas Nelson. Nelson Books and Thomas Nelson are registered trademarks of HarperCollins Christian Publishing, Inc.

Published in association with Yates & Yates, www.yates2.com.

Thomas Nelson titles may be purchased in bulk for educational, business, fundraising, or sales promotional use. For information, please e-mail SpecialMarkets@ThomasNelson.com.

ISBN 978-1-4002-3197-3 (HC)

Printed in the United States of America

21 22 23 24 25 LSC 10 9 8 7 6 5 4 3 2 1

Contents

Letter from Author

Family team,

Most of us want to "do family" the best we can. We each bring a very particular experience of family to the table, so when we have families of our own, we hang on to what we want to keep from our childhoods and reject what we *don't* want to keep. But I've learned that the work of developing a healthy family is a bit stickier than picking and choosing from a menu of the past. Especially in the West, families are shaped by forces we may not even notice—until we do. Until we experience pain and heartbreak over how today's family hasn't lived up to our expectations. Or our hopes. Or the promises that our culture has held out as tantalizing fool's gold in front of us.

Powerful forces in our society—a hyper-focus on the individual and an insatiable desire to consume—have taken control of our families. They've misled us into thinking the nuclear family is the pinnacle of existence when that ideal has crumbled under its false weight. These forces have carved out more influence than any parent can and even more than the church has.

As Alyssa and I have worked alongside the passionate "family changers" who are part of our Family Teams initiative, we've glimpsed how fulfilling and life-giving family can be. Moms and dads and grandparents are taking back their families, and what we're seeing is beautiful. It's biblical. It's majorly influencing the world. And it probably doesn't look the way you'd expect. That's why I'm so glad you are on this journey with us. Even though the enemy of God's vision for our families is insidious and mighty, we're confident we can take back our families with intention.

Team, this is *doable*. And it's important.

This guide is meant to help you process and apply the ideas you're discovering in *Take Back Your Family*. Each week, for fifty-two weeks, you'll dig into a "big idea" that can become the seed of a conversation for your family to have together. Maybe you'll choose Tuesday night as your gathering time for cracking open this book and tossing out the ideas in your living room. Or Sunday afternoons on your back porch. Whenever and wherever you do it, I'm inviting you to observe how your family operates—and to learn how to become a family team. Together, you'll decide how your family will flourish. (For referencing and reflection in years to come, you may want to dedicate a separate notebook to journal comments as you go along.)

At the end of the handbook, I encourage you to complete a Family Summit, which will revisit and analyze the past year so you can create a vision for the next year. It's a powerful tool my own family uses.

The cultural forces that have led us to a broken hope have also disrupted the healthy, flourishing families for which we were made. But families who are choosing to opt in to something so much better are tasting—and sharing!—the goodness of God.

Fellow coaches, we can do this.

Jefferson

WEEK 1

Big Idea: God's design for families is intergenerational.

The vision of family Alyssa and I witnessed in Jerusalem at a traditional Shabbat dinner wasn't biblical just because we ate food in Bible-land. Among other reasons, it was biblical because it was multigenerational. We witnessed grandparents, and toddlers, and parents, and teens-who-weren't-surly valuing the connection among them. We were, quite frankly, baffled. But it helped us to notice that God's good design for their families, and ours, is intergenerational. Although intergenerational families took a hit in the United States in the middle of the twentieth century, I'm convinced there is untapped richness in God's good design.

- Where have you seen a family flourishing because they have chosen to live intergenerationally?
- What are the particular ways in which your family has missed out on the blessings of being an intergenerational family?

- How have the generations of your family thrived in the moments and seasons when you've done life together?
- **FOR YOUNGER TEAM MEMBERS:** One by one, think about each of your grandparents. What's your favorite thing about each one?

Game Plan

This week, intentionally engage with someone outside of the generations living in your home. Ideally, this much-older or much-younger person would be a family member. If that's not possible, reach out to someone else in need of welcome.

NOTES

WEEK 2

Big Idea: The family is where each member discovers his or her God-given identity.

Wrestling to put my finger on what was different about the families we were meeting in Israel, I asked my friend Jeremy a question: Why did they seem so radically different—stronger, happier—than families I'd encountered in the United States? He explained, "They see the family as one of the main places to find an identity." At the time, everyone I knew derived identity from education, employment, successes, and line items on a résumé. They sure weren't defining themselves by their families.

- Can you think of another family wherein each member is discovering his or her God-given identity? Give specific examples.
- Did you—or did you not—come to know your God-given identity within the context of your family? Describe your experience.
- If you've not experienced a family in which members derived

identity from one another, where have you seen it occurring in literature or film? (Just not *The Godfather*. Try harder.)

- **FOR YOUNGER TEAM MEMBERS:** What is one quality or characteristic about *you* that is special? How has God made you unique? (Your parents can help if you get stuck!)

Game Plan

This week, set aside time to reflect on the identity of each member of your family team. Specifically, focus on the unique gifts God has given to each individual. (And keep a record of them, so you can return to take a peek in a decade or two!)

NOTES

DIG DEEPER . . .

I played baseball as a child, and my children play sports now. I've been coached and have been a coach, so I know the importance of studying the players. I think it's equally as important to study the players on the family team. Alyssa and I use our family's scouting reports to note the different roles each person plays in our family—and to dig deep into what makes each person tick. That way, we are intentionally looking for how our family can be as well-balanced and whole as possible—ready to be a family on mission.

Spend some time creating a scouting report for each member of your team using the questions below. Put the reports in a safe place—tucked into the back of this book, or maybe in a cabinet over the fridge—because you'll revisit these in six months!

1. What's their role on the team?
2. How are they wired or gifted?
3. How or where do they need the most support?
4. What activities do we need to prioritize for them to flourish?
5. What is the best way to spend one-on-one time with them?
6. When do they come most alive?

WEEK 3

Big Idea: The family is the primary vehicle for bringing blessing and goodness into the world.

Jeremy's observations about the way people "do family" in Israel really was eye-opening for me. Truly life-changing. Because he also named families as "the primary vehicle for bringing blessing and goodness into the world." That little seed took root in me and has not yet stopped growing and producing fruit. The idea has revolutionized my own family as well as the message I'm sharing with other families.

We'll continue to dig into this further because it's *big*.

- How have you seen another family bring blessing and goodness into the world? Share some of the specific ways they've done it.
- Do you think your family has been missing out on opportunities to bring blessing and goodness into the world? Explore that.
- God executed his plan to bring blessing and goodness into the world through the family of Abraham, Isaac, and Jacob. What

other families in Scripture lived out this calling to bring blessing and goodness into the world? Specifically, how did they do it?

- **FOR YOUNGER TEAM MEMBERS:** Can you think of a family you know that loves and serves others as a team?

Game Plan

Decide how your family team will bring blessing and goodness into the world this week. Surprise birthday party for the widower next door? (Who cares if it's not actually his birthday?) Icy cold water bottles for strangers? Make the challenge your own, and have fun with it.

NOTES

WEEK 4

Big Idea: The family is a unit of change in the kingdom of God.

The Cracker Barrel meal Alyssa and I shared with Jeremy and his wife, April, was a game changer for me. It felt like everything I'd previously thought about marriage and family was deconstructed and reconstructed over delicious cheese grits. And one of the things that unlocked inside me was the keen awareness that God uses families to accomplish his purposes.

I was familiar with the individual heroes of the faith—Moses, Esther, David, Mary, etc.—but when I returned to their stories, I saw how they weren't lone rangers at all: they served God in conjunction with their families.

- Whether your example is a mom and a child—like my early family—or a family of nine, how have you witnessed a family functioning together to usher in God's kingdom?
- Many families seem to function as individuals with one electric

bill. In what specific ways do you recognize the scourge of individualism at work in your family?

- How does your family work together as agents of God's kingdom today?
- **FOR YOUNGER TEAM MEMBERS:** Can you think of one family from the Bible that helped others? (If you're stuck, your parents will help!)

Game Plan

Notice one place in which your family team has not been functioning as a unit. Then strategize how to improve that place. Is your student athlete doing travel league alone? Does Dad invite little helpers into his yardwork? Be creative.

NOTES

WEEK 5

Big Idea: The family is a hub around which other spokes turn.

The kind of "home" I was beginning to see through Jeremy and April's family was a type of a hub around which everything else revolved. Rather than a mere pitstop—where everyone fueled up only to return to the world—the home was at the center of their lives. Spirituality wasn't found in the church building; it was found at home. Economic activity wasn't located in an office building; it was rooted at home. The best meals didn't have to happen at restaurants; they happened at home.

- When you look around at families you respect, which ones function as hubs with spokes? Describe, in detail, how those families operate.
- How have you externalized part of your life, or your family's life, to someplace outside of the home? Try to identify places with little or no connection to the life of the family that have decentralized your home.

- In what ways have you succeeded in creating a home that is a hub for the life of its members?
- **FOR YOUNGER TEAM MEMBERS:** What is your favorite meal that your family eats together at home?

Game Plan

This week, identify one way in which life outside the home is disconnected from the life of the family. Then determine how you can be more creative about integrating what has disintegrated.

NOTES

WEEK 6

Big Idea: Multigenerational family teams on mission are God's good idea.

If you were raised in a family without a missional vision, the idea likely sounds a bit strange at first, like it did to me. Many American families today are about hustling to make money so they can buy the things that make each individual happy and, ultimately, liberate each individual *from* the family so they can make more money to buy more happy-making things. But the families God chose to use throughout Scripture had a sense of mission and purpose.

- Where have you seen a multigenerational family team being on mission with God?
- In your childhood family or current family, what is one small way that your family has embraced being on mission together?
- As you think about the kind of mission for which your family

might be particularly suited, what comes to mind? What is your family uniquely equipped to do?

- **FOR YOUNGER TEAM MEMBERS:** What is one cool thing that one of your grandparents knows how to do? (It might happen in the garage, in the kitchen, in an art studio, in the garden, etc.)

Game Plan

Discuss the ways your family is uniquely suited to be on mission. Notice the gifts and passions of individuals and find where they overlap. Record your dreams about how God is calling your family to engage with the world God loves.

NOTES

WEEK 7

Big Idea: Elderly members of our culture and families are indispensable.

In a culture that values youth, fitness, and beauty, older members of its society are too often neglected and ignored. It's not that we despise them outright; it's more that we just don't *see* them. When we pass an elderly man in the grocery store clutching his shopping cart and grocery list, or when we stand behind a stooped, gray-haired woman at the bank, we've not been coached to recognize those individuals as precious, beloved, valuable, unique individuals created in the image of God. More often we dismiss their value and miss out on the rich gifts they offer.

- As you notice other families, how do you see younger members honoring the indispensable contributions of older members? Be specific.
- In your extended family, how have elderly people been undervalued or cut off from the life of younger generations?

- In what ways has your family honored and celebrated the gifts its older members bring?
- **FOR YOUNGER TEAM MEMBERS:** Together, as a family, try to think of the oldest person you know. What is special about this precious person?

Game Plan

Pause this week to invest in discovering more about the older members of your family. Whether through a visit or video call, take time to listen and learn from your family's eldest members.

NOTES

WEEK 8

Big Idea: Family is where the most vulnerable are welcome and protected.

Too often those who identify as "pro family" have idealized something other than the biblical vision of family. The iconic *Leave It to Beaver* nuclear family that revolves around safety, consumption, and individual happiness is a far cry from God's good plan. Instead, the ancient vision for family was much more robust! It was a web of relationships where the vulnerable and downtrodden, young and old, were welcomed and protected.

- Have you noticed another family welcoming and protecting the most vulnerable? What are the specific ways they do this?
- As you think about the family as a refuge for those in need, can you see opportunities you missed to open your family to others?
- In what ways has your family, early or current, been a place of welcome and protection for those in need?

- **FOR YOUNGER TEAM MEMBERS:** People who are vulnerable might need a little extra love and care to stay safe and healthy. Is there anyone you know who could use a little extra love from your family?

Game Plan

Ask God to bring one person to mind—from your extended family, your church, or your neighborhood—who is in need of welcome. This week, find one way to integrate into your family the person who's been marginalized.

NOTES

DIG DEEPER . . .

God's plan to care for the lonely happens through you and your family! Invite your family to think of those in your orbit—family, neighbors, church, or school—who might be blessed by an invitation into your home. Consider some folks who may need extra love and care:

A person who is elderly: ___________________
A person without family nearby: ___________________
An immigrant: ___________________
A person with an intellectual or physical disability:___________________
A parent raising children solo: ___________________
A single adult living alone: ___________________
A person who might be a bit awkward socially: ___________________
A person with a difficult home life: ___________________
A person experiencing financial instability: ___________________
A person enduring illness or injury: ___________________
A person grieving a loss (death, divorce, unemployment): ___________________

As you look over this list, help your family decide whom you'd like to invite over to share a meal. Aim to invite this person within the next week. When you welcome one of these precious ones whom God loves, offer them the seat of honor at your table. Then, after spending time together, invite your family members to name what they appreciate about your guest!

CAUTION: Don't try to care for *everyone*. Instead, focus on *someone*. Just take the next step by inviting someone to share a meal this week.

WEEK 9

Big Idea: Family is a place to rest and be known.

God's answer to loneliness, as voiced in Psalm 68:6, is to set the lonely in families—and we can get really creative with this. Maybe we invite an international college student to share dinner with our family each week. Maybe we welcome an older single woman to become "auntie" to our children. Or we might even visit someone in prison who is hungry for company. When we open our homes and families in these ways, we make room for others, and for ourselves, to rest and be known.

- When you've been a guest in the homes of others, have you experienced a family that felt like a place to rest and be known? Were there specific practices that made this possible?
- In what ways did your earliest family fail to know, cherish, and reflect upon who you really are? Or how did your earliest family succeed in this regard?
- How is your family making room for its members to rest and be known?

- **FOR YOUNGER TEAM MEMBERS:** Is there anyone you know who is "like family" to you? If not, who might you like to invite into your home?

Game Plan

Each night this week, choose one family member to take the seat of honor. (Consider creating a special paper crown or silly hat. A scepter wouldn't be unheard of.) Let each family member name what they notice and appreciate about each night's honored member.

NOTES

WEEK 10

Big Idea: The healthiest families run more like farms than like factories.

Before the Industrial Revolution, moms and dads and grandparents all "worked from home." In agrarian societies—the dominant pre-industrial model across human cultures—home was the hub where the whole family worked side by side. Until very recently, the household was the center of both production and identity: the place where work and family were integrated.

- Whether or not they live on an actual farm (although they might!), what respectable family have you observed functioning like a farm?
- In your experience of family until now, how has yours functioned more like a factory than a farm?
- Notice and name the ways that your family functions more like a farm than a factory.

- **FOR YOUNGER TEAM MEMBERS:** Who do you know who works from home? (And do you think you'd like to do that one day?)

Game Plan

As you notice the ways in which your family is factorylike—possibly out of necessity—identify one way to integrate what happens outside the home with life inside the home.

NOTES

WEEK 11

Big Idea: Every family can function as a team on mission.

By rejecting the idealized caricature of the nuclear family that includes mom, dad, boy, girl, dog, and picket fence, we recognize that missional families look all kinds of ways. Families led by a single parent are on mission. Families that include a person with a disability or chronic illness are blessing others. Families that have been broken by divorce are being used as agents of God's kingdom. Families with two parents leading the team are living missionally.

- Scrapping the iconic mom-dad-two-kids-and-a-dog family, where have you seen a more uniquely configured family serving as a team on mission?
- Have the particular circumstances of your family—single parent, divorced, blended, special needs, chronic illness, adoptive, foster, etc.—ever interfered with missional living? (Consider either real hurdles or imaginary ones.)
- Now flip it. How do the unique circumstances of your family

make you *particularly* suited for living on mission? How can God use your family because of the way it's unique?

- **FOR YOUNGER TEAM MEMBERS:** How does your family work together to love and serve others?

Game Plan

Whether or not living on mission is already part of your family culture, identify one way this week you will reach beyond yourselves as builders of God's kingdom.

NOTES

WEEK 12

Big Idea: The reintegration of families across generations is healthy.

According to the Pew Research Center, 21 percent of the American population lived in multigenerational households in 1951. But as younger generations began peeling off to live independently, often pursuing financial opportunities in other cities, that number dropped to 12 percent in 1980. A recent census shows that by 2016 that number had climbed back up to 20 percent of Americans living in multigenerational households.[1] While some would identify this as "regression," this type of reintegration is actually something to celebrate.

- Although we see families splitting apart all around us, when have you seen a family reintegrate—either by virtue of choice or circumstance—across generational lines?
- Notice and reflect on the points at which your family has

separated, due to job opportunity, housing opportunity, nursing home care, or other reasons.

- If applicable, how has your family reintegrated? (For example widowed, ill, or elderly parent moving in; child moving back home after college)
- **FOR YOUNGER TEAM MEMBERS:** If you could choose someone (or *someones*!) from your extended family to join your household, whom would you pick?

Game Plan

Even if no pressing need for reintegration has presented itself—memory loss, unexpected illness, disability, etc.—consider whether there is a way in which family reintegration could make your family team more whole.

NOTES

WEEK 13

Big Idea: Families are made for legacy building.

Maybe you've heard a family you know bragging that they've become empty nesters. Our culture celebrates kicking our baby birds out of the nest! We even count it as a failure when they return. But the family God chooses in Scripture—descendants of Abraham, Isaac, and Jacob—is designed to build legacy through the generations. We were wired to build things that last, and although we often seek to "build" through our work and business projects, family legacy is what we were made for. Together your family builds legacy—something that lasts beyond generations.

- As you noodle on all the families you've known, consider which family has set an example of legacy building. How have they built legacy together?
- What are the ways in which your family, past or current, has celebrated the amputation of its members?

- In what particular ways have you purposefully integrated generations into the legacy, or the inheritance, you're building?
- **FOR YOUNGER TEAM MEMBERS:** As you think about yourself getting older, what do you imagine being the good things about living at home as a young adult? Which things might be hard?

Game Plan

Consider where your family is today—the seasons and ages of each member—and think forward twenty years. Now think forward fifty years. What will you begin to do this week to build the legacy your family's younger members will inherit?

NOTES

WEEK 14

Big Idea: Families centered around consumption diminish their members.

On the "minimal" inheritance his children will receive, Bill Gates explained, "We want to strike a balance where they have the freedom to do anything but not a lot of money showered on them so they could go out and do nothing."[2] Insightful, right?! When we use the resources we have to equip our children for mission, everyone wins. Yet when we use the resources we have to help our children consume, everyone loses. A family culture that celebrates consumption disserves, stunts, and limits its members.

- Without being unkind, where have you seen a family whose members were diminished because they focused on consumption? (This one might be a family you've seen in the media.)
- You don't have to be Bill Gates to use your resources thoughtfully.

What are the ways in which you or your family have squandered resources on excess?

- How are you creatively using the resources with which you've been entrusted to benefit—and equip your children to benefit—the world God loves?
- **FOR YOUNGER TEAM MEMBERS:** If someone gave your family one million dollars to help others, how would *you* choose to use it? (And what if it was twenty dollars?)

Game Plan

This week, choose one new way for your family to direct some of its resources to benefit others.

NOTES

DIG DEEPER . . .

A secret some families have discovered is that when we intentionally reduce the excess *stuff* in our lives, two things happen: First, we discover freedom. Second, once we've tasted that freedom, we're less inclined to purchase more stuff to replace the old. Win-win!

Set aside a Saturday to get rid of the unnecessary stuff your family has accumulated. As you discuss who is best-suited to tackle each space, divide your family into work teams, pairing each child who needs extra help with an adult. (Obviously each team will choose an awesome team name.)

Coach your teams to ask two questions as they evaluate items in your home:

- Does this item help us create the culture we want in our home?
- Do we love or use it?

If the answers are "no," enjoy the freedom of releasing these items!

Ask the artist in your family to create signs for five collection piles you'll create in a common space:

- **SELL:** items to be sold
- **SHARE:** items to be shared with someone who can use them

- **REUSE:** items to be donated to a thrift or reuse store
- **RECYCLE:** paper, plastic, or metal items to be recycled
- **TRASH:** items whose only home is in the trash

Assign teams to each of the following areas:

Kitchen: ____________________

Bathrooms: ____________________

Living Room: ____________________

Dining Room: ____________________

Master Bedroom: ____________________

Other Bedroom/s: ____________________

Laundry/Utility Room: ____________________

Other (office, playroom, guest room, etc.): ____________________

Basement or Attic: ____________________

Garage: ____________________

Celebrate your accomplishments with a meal out that everyone will enjoy!

WEEK 15

Big Idea: A family is a relational home.

In Durham, North Carolina, a very unique family has recently been built. Through conversation and prayer, a single woman, a single man, and a married couple discerned that God was leading them to share their lives with adult friends in their community who lived with intellectual disabilities. By God's grace and the support of many, the four welcomed three adults of differing ages, abilities, races, and socioeconomic classes to share a house with them. Today—five years and two children later!—this diverse crew, knit into a relational home, is a family.

- When you think of family as a "relational home" rather than a unit of people related by blood and marriage, what specific family comes to mind?
- As you consider your earliest family, was there a way in which it functioned as something other than a relational home (e.g., parking garage, daycare center, factory, launchpad to independence)?

- As of today, how does your family intentionally function as a relational home?
- **FOR YOUNGER TEAM MEMBERS:** Can you think of a living situation where people who aren't related by blood have become family? (Your parents can help you answer.)

Game Plan

Notice each of the relationships between members of your family team. Identify one that can be strengthened, and plan one engagement to enjoy this week that will help move you toward that purpose.

NOTES

WEEK 16

Big Idea: "Team" is God's good design for the family.

It wasn't a secret to me that the hyper-individualism of our culture has hindered the flourishing of strong families. But the language of *team* finally brought it home for me because I understood how a team should work. On a team, the hotdog who puts himself and his success before the other members of the team is a liability, not an asset. When you think of "Team Trinity," each member—Father, Son, and Holy Spirit—makes the other members look good! Individualism is about me and what I am doing. Team is about us and what we are doing.

- Think about the strongest, healthiest team you know. It might be a local high school team or a professional one you've read about. How does this team function like a family?
- As you reflect on your early family and your current one, where do you see "me" getting in the way of "we"?
- Note and name the ways your family is functioning like a team today.

- **FOR YOUNGER TEAM MEMBERS:** On a team, everyone works together as a unit. Is there an activity in which your family participates where you work to accomplish something together?

Game Plan

Plan a game night with another family that approximates the ages and stages of your family members. Make some "Team Johnson" T-shirts or make up a silly family cheer. Engage together as a team and work together to win.

NOTES

WEEK 17

Big Idea: Your family is called to participate in a general mission and a particular mission.

Every family is called to the *general* mission of building God's kingdom. But your family has a unique combination of people, gifts, wiring, and passions that is unlike any other family that has ever dwelled on the planet. (But, hey, no pressure.) Ask God to show you the particular mission to which your family is being called. Maybe you've been given a heart to share the good news with those who have never heard it. Or maybe God has brought together a team of justice warriors. Notice how your family has been uniquely designed to execute a particular mission in the world God loves.

- Think about other families you know on mission. Which family has a clear sense of their particular mission? Share how they live it out.
- If the family in which you were raised was missional, celebrate

that. If it was not, consider how your circumstances got in the way of blessing others.

- Today, what are the ways your family is already on mission?
- **FOR YOUNGER TEAM MEMBERS:** What do you notice that makes your family a little different from other families? How is yours special and unique?

Game Plan

Put a big piece of butcher paper out on the table. Now make a grid. Across the top, list the names of family team members. And in a column on the left, name categories like wiring, personality, gift, strength, skill, passion, experience. Then, as a family, fill in the blocks that identify what is unique about each member. Do you see any themes emerging that suggest your family's particular mission?

NOTES

WEEK 18

Big Idea: God heals family trauma.

Back in chapter 1, I mentioned the adverse childhood experience (ACE) score assigned to those who experienced trauma in childhood. What each of us experienced as youths doesn't stay in the past. We carry it with us. And for some of us, it's a heavy load. It's not uncommon for some of those old hurts to be exposed when we marry and have our own children. Those wounds have shaped how we understand family, and God longs to heal the pain we carry when we offer it to him. Healing is a process, and as we offer our hurts to the One who cares, God is faithful to heal and redeem.

- Can you think of a family—either one you know personally, one you've heard about, or one you've only read about—in which God has healed old hurts? Describe the family that comes to mind.
- Being very gentle with yourself, notice the adverse childhood experiences you endured: physical, emotional, or sexual abuse; physical or emotional neglect; household dysfunctions including

mental illness, incarcerated relatives, abused parents, substance abuse, divorce; etc. Share as you feel comfortable. (If this conversation isn't helpful to your young children, you can invite them into a conversation about the kinds of dangers other children might face.)

- Share how God has either healed your own hurts or how God has healed the hurts of others.
- **FOR YOUNGER TEAM MEMBERS:** You know what it's like when a cut or bruise on your body heals. Ask an older family member if he or she can tell you how God healed his or her *heart* from old hurts.

Game Plan

As you notice hurts in need of healing, offer them to God this week. You know this isn't a one-and-done task. Healing takes time. Consider using a journal to record your need, your prayers, God's responses, and scriptures that are meaningful on your healing journey. Pray with your family for God to protect and heal those in need.

NOTES

WEEK 19

Big Idea: Integrated families form a functioning, unified whole.

The Bible has a little somethin' to say about the integration of team members. In the body, the eye can't tell the hand, "I don't need you, sucker." And the head can't tell the feet, "Get out of here. I don't need you!" (See 1 Corinthians 12.) Instead, the members *depend* upon one another in order to do their jobs; the hand raises a pair of glasses to the eyes, or the feet take the head where it needs to go. Also, out of no selfish interest, they have concern for the well-being of one another.

- In a culture where families are zipping off in all directions, what family have you seen functioning as a unified whole?
- What was it (while growing up) or what is it (today) that kept or keeps your family from functioning as a unified whole? This isn't about pointing fingers but rather about noticing practices and patterns.

- How do you see your family functioning as a unified whole? (It might be super simple: riding in the van to church together or visiting Grandma's at Christmas.)
- **FOR YOUNGER TEAM MEMBERS:** In a body, the hand needs the eye in order to do its work. In your family, how does one member support the other one, helping that person do what he or she was made to do?

Game Plan

If your family is thriving by functioning as a unified whole, plan a special activity you can share to celebrate that. If you're not, choose a weekly ritual—involving play, service, study, or creativity—that you can enjoy as a unified whole.

NOTES

WEEK 20

Big Idea: Members of teams need each other.

If you're wondering what it looks like to be a family on mission, look at teams. Teams are *on mission*. They know what the mission is, they keep it in view, and they prepare themselves to accomplish that defined mission. Even though you'll occasionally see a player showboating, every member knows how to work together to accomplish the mission. No one player can do it alone; teams need each other to win the prize. Too many families behave as if their members don't need one another, and such individualism threatens the mission.

- As you think about families that embody mutuality, where do you see them needing one another?
- As you look at your family culture today, where do you see hints of individualism that could hurt the team? (Be gentle with your answers. Be kind. You're on the same team here.)
- Do you recognize your healthy dependence on and interdependence with one another? Describe these dynamics.

- **FOR YOUNGER TEAM MEMBERS:** When one player scores a home run, the whole team celebrates! What recent "win" of one member can your whole family celebrate together?

Game Plan

What is one specific way you can resist and rebuild one of the places where you recognize the corruption of individualism in your team? (Hint: Be creative! Which team member can contribute to that area in a way that thwarts individualism?)

NOTES

DIG DEEPER . . .

Teams function best when everyone works together. And teams really thrive when players have the opportunity to contribute their strengths and gifts!

Pause to notice the unique qualities that each member brings to your team. Whether you're doing chores around the house or reaching out to meet needs in your community, noticing and honoring these gifts make your team stronger.

What strengths does each team member bring to your family? Jot each person's name beside one or two strengths, or offer your own below.

Relationships with Others

- Protective
- Nurturing
- Motivating and inspiring
- Sensitive to needs
- Encouraging
- Generous
- Communicates well

Natural Wiring / Ways of Thinking

- Right-brained, creative

- Left-brained, analytical
- Innovative, problem solving
- Inquisitive, perceptive, observant
- Organized
- Aesthetically inclined, recognizes beauty

Vision

- Focused, goal-oriented
- Careful, detail-oriented

Leadership and Execution

- Leads well, communicates vision
- Plays well with others, works hard

Other Strengths and Gifts

-
-
-
-

WEEK 21

Big Idea: Family teams are fundamentally different from clubs.

If you've participated in a club, it was likely in middle school or high school. French club, anyone? Math club? Chess club? Clubs are made up of individuals who band together to enjoy a shared activity. The grown-up version of a club might be the swim and tennis club. There's no great purpose or vision involved: just the common interest. Teams, however, are distinctively corporate. A team has a clear objective and is knit together by a shared identity and mission. The family that functions like a club is at risk, because it was designed to be so much more. Families that function like teams, though, thrive as they share a common mission.

- Without being unkind, have you noticed another family that functions more like a club than a team? (Families in literature, television, and movies are fair game for this one!)

- Do you recognize how your family, past or present, shrunk itself to operate more like a club than a team? Describe what you've noticed.
- Today, how is your family operating like a team that's knit together by a shared identity and is accomplishing a mission together?
- **FOR YOUNGER TEAM MEMBERS:** If you think about the members of your family team as a baseball team, what *position* does each member play and why? (If your family has another favorite sport, you can use that one as a framework instead!)

Game Plan

If you recognize more of a club mentality than a team mentality in your family, make it plain to everyone that your vision for family is "team." Get some big letters at a craft store to decorate and post in your home: "We are a team." Or place sticky note reminders in every bathroom. Communicate your vision clearly!

NOTES

WEEK 22

Big Idea: Family team leaders have the DNA of the best coaches.

I count it a great honor to have played high school baseball for Coach Kuykendall. He had success on the field, but more importantly, he impacted the lives of boys who were becoming men. If you've ever had the gift of playing for a good coach, you know how formative that relationship can be. A coach sees the potential in you that you don't yet see in yourself. And he or she encourages you to become your best self. A coach knows how to nurture that potential. He or she knows when to push you harder, and when to let you breathe. And the leaders of your family team are meant to have the same impact.

- As you think about the leaders of the healthiest families you know, in what ways do they function like good coaches of sports teams?
- If you're reading this, you're likely a coach for your family team.

What did you learn about leadership from the coach in the family in which you were raised?

- Based upon what you learned from your role models and what you're learning in *Take Back Your Family*, how are you functioning like one of the best coaches?
- **FOR YOUNGER TEAM MEMBERS:** Who in your family has played for a great coach? Ask that member to describe what made that person a strong coach.

Game Plan

Notice where your coaching game could be improved. Do your players need more encouragement? More discipline? More Slurpees? Identify one tactical move to implement this week that will strengthen your team members.

NOTES

WEEK 23

Big Idea: Individuals depend on themselves; teams depend on each other.

Alyssa and I experienced a learning curve as we began our parenting journey. And by "learning curve," I mean she felt like she was parenting alone when I was gone. Guilty. For those of us who weren't raised in a culture of mutual interdependence, the shift from depending on one's self to depending on others is a steep curve. That doesn't mean we'll suddenly become dependent on someone else; it simply means we need to be weaned off our addiction to independence. (In this story I was the wean-ee, as it were.)

- When have you seen, or experienced firsthand, a family where all the members depend on one another?
- What were the quiet signals, or outright announcements, you heard growing up that taught you independence was to be prized?

- Identify the ways your current family team works interdependently (mutually depending on one another for support).
- **FOR YOUNGER TEAM MEMBERS:** How do different members of your family *depend* on one another? (Ask your parents to help, if you need it.)

Game Plan

One family made the very un-American choice to go from owning two cars to owning one car. It required more interdependence, but they made it work. Can your family make a similar simple choice to increase interdependence and decrease independence?

NOTES

WEEK 24

Big Idea: The lie that a father's main job is to "financially provide" harms families.

When Alyssa expressed her concern about my absence from the home, my go-to defense was: "I'm providing." Provision wasn't some lame excuse either. I'd been taught, and likely you've been taught, that it's *noble*. But I've become convinced that no lie has been more destructive to Christian fatherhood than this one. One reason it's poison is because it allows a breadwinner who provides food, clothing, and shelter to bail on any other family responsibility. And it's also used as an excuse for fathers to be absent from the family. When bodily needs are met, what families need most is the provision of presence, grace, gentleness, compassion, leadership, and more.

- Can you think of a family you know that has suffered because the father was exiled from the family so that he could "provide"?

- As you look back through the generations of your own family, do you recognize this lie at work?
- If your family includes a father, how are you actively combatting this lie today?
- **FOR YOUNGER TEAM MEMBERS:** When your father is at home, what do you most enjoy doing together? (Or it could be another person who's bringing home a paycheck.)

Game Plan

Identify one shift you could make in your family to make room for the father to have the freedom to be engaged in ways other than financial provision. It can be small, like taking a teen on his morning run, or it could be large, like a couple sharing financial responsibility for the family's needs. Find what makes the most sense for *your* family.

NOTES

WEEK 25

Big Idea: Patterns of communication predict a team's success.

The experiments of Alex Pentland—using badge lanyards with devices monitoring interpersonal variables during communication—have proven that patterns of communication predict a team's success. He found that the most effective leaders naturally used what he calls "honest signals"—such as eye contact and energy and vocal pitch—to signal, "You are safe here." What we can glean from these findings is that our style of communication, even when we're communicating unconsciously, matters more than we realize when it comes to our family team.

- What successful family have you encountered in which the members were strong communicators?
- Can you identify patterns of communication in your childhood home that you feel diminished the success of that team?

(Hint: While you may have experienced blatant rage or shame language, many damaging communication patterns are much more subtle. Notice what your gut is telling you.)

- What communication choices are you making to enhance the success of your team?
- **FOR YOUNGER TEAM MEMBERS:** Try to tell your mom or dad about your favorite game or sport while their eyes are locked on their phone. Then have the same conversation eyeball-to-eyeball. What's different?

Game Plan

Choose one element of effective communication that your team will choose to implement. Maybe you value eye contact. Maybe you make a policy of no interrupting in order to honor other members. What communication styles are going to benefit your team?

NOTES

WEEK 26

Big Idea: The unique strengths of each family team member are celebrated.

In the second week of this handbook, you had the opportunity to create a scouting report for each member of your team. A scouting report is a mini textbook on your players that helps you make informed decisions about the team. While a typical scouting report might include stats like height, weight, speed, and strength, it also includes more nuanced information like, "What does this player tend to do when scared or in a hard situation?" or "How does this player act when he strikes out?" or "What are her tendencies under pressure?" The strong family coach knows all this and more. The coach knows what makes their hearts light up, how they're wired, and what their weaknesses are. Family scouting reports serve the players and serve the team.

- Do you know a family who has done a good job of noticing

and celebrating the unique strengths of each family member? Describe this team.

- Did anyone in your early life take note of the unique gifts and strengths you'd been given by God? How did that person make you feel?
- How are you already identifying and naming your team members' strengths and weaknesses?
- **FOR YOUNGER TEAM MEMBERS:** Go around the circle of family members and name *one strength* that you love or admire in each person.

Game Plan

Let each member report about whether they feel they've been given the opportunity to use their gifts as a member of the team.

NOTES

DIG DEEPER . . .

Six months ago you created a scouting report for each member of your family's team. Pull out these scouting reports and pause to notice who those individuals are *today*.

As you review the answers from your last scouting report, ask three more questions:

- Do we notice any growth or change in this individual?
- Has this individual had opportunities in the last six months to contribute using their unique strengths?
- Do we need to do anything differently for this individual to flourish?

Now it's time to create an updated scouting report for each individual:

1. What's their role on the team?
2. How are they wired or gifted?
3. How or where do they need the most support?
4. What activities do we need to prioritize for them to flourish?
5. What is the best way to spend one-on-one time with them?
6. When do they come most alive?

WEEK 27

Big Idea: Adding team members makes our team stronger.

Too often, when children are preparing to receive a new sibling by birth or adoption, we speak of the transition as a loss rather than a win for them. "She won't be the star of the show anymore." "He won't have his parents' undivided attention." "She'll have to share her toys." "They'll have to make room for one more." I want to push back against that harmful narrative and flip it. Adding young or old family members to our team should make us want to shout with joy. We should throw a party and post a banner that brags, "Our team just got better!" That's how we have narrated the growth of our own family, and I encourage others to hop aboard the "more not less" train!

- Can you think of a family who added team members and became stronger? Be creative as you consider this one.
- What were the quiet or spoken ways that your first family implied that adding new members was a loss and not a win for the team?

- How have you created a new story that celebrates the gift of adding special, new members into the mix?
- **FOR YOUNGER TEAM MEMBERS:** Who is the most recent addition to your family team? Ask everyone to name why your family is stronger because of that person!

Game Plan

You don't need to conceive a new human to celebrate growing families. Do you know a family with five kids who just announced they're having a sixth "oops" baby? Is a family in your church welcoming a recently widowed grandparent to live with them? Throw a party to celebrate someone else's new addition.

NOTES

WEEK 28

Big Idea: Sibling relationships are intentional, not accidental.

It's my hunch, and others have confirmed it, that an American myth suggests that siblings—or rather the relationships between siblings—are inconsequential. By some random luck of the draw, brothers and sisters end up living under the same roof without meaning or purpose. That's the vibe I get from many families who have been twisted by individualism. We're quick to accept that sibling rivalry is a real (and expected) dynamic, but we're slow to name the ways relationships between siblings are meant to be particularly meaningful. As family coaches, it's up to us to name the inestimable value of those relationships and to equip siblings to be intentional about developing and maintaining those lifelong bonds.

- As you've surveyed other families, which sibling relationships have you really admired? What made them special?
- Growing up, what was your experience with sibling relationships? What messages did you receive about their value?

- How is your family supporting the bond between each unique sibling pair on the team?
- **FOR YOUNGER TEAM MEMBERS:** Tell each of your siblings your favorite thing about them! (If you don't have siblings, ask your parent to tell you about their childhood relationship with a sibling.)

Game Plan

If you haven't yet been intentional about nurturing sibling bonds in your family, there's no better time to start than right now. Help each sibling pair plan a one-on-one time this week.

NOTES

WEEK 29

Big Idea: The healthiest family teams know who they are.

When restaurateur Danny Meyer learned a guest had not been treated well at one of his restaurants, he temporarily closed up shop and said, "This is not who we are." The restaurants would not move forward until they decided, as a team, who they were. After an intense and challenging weekend summit, team members left having established five clear priorities. Some of those priorities flew in the face of conventional wisdom, of "how things have always been done," but they established a culture of excellence that continues to this day.

- Can you describe one family you know who has a very clear sense of identity?
- If your earliest family had penned a one-sentence mission statement, what do you think it would have said? Who did your family understand itself to be?
- Today, what level of understanding does each member of your

family team have about your family's identity? Does each understand *who you are*?

- **FOR YOUNGER TEAM MEMBERS:** If your family was a book and you had to choose a title for that book, what would it be?

Game Plan

This week, discuss your family's identity and define who you are. It might be a single-sentence mission statement or a list of four or five priorities. It doesn't have to be set in stone forever, but answer the question, "Why are we here?"

NOTES

WEEK 30

Big Idea: A team fights a common enemy together.

Gilman High's football coach Joe Ehrmann was intentional about shaping his players on and off the field. The team's goal was to beat their rival and win the division championship, but the team's *purpose*, according to Ehrmann, was to combat what he called "false masculinity" in its three components: athletic ability, sexual conquest, and economic success. Through his words, actions, and coaching, Ehrmann equipped his team to fight an invisible enemy that was coming for them. Ehrmann was crystal clear about the purpose of the team.

- Do you know a family team that has battled a common enemy together? Illness? Calamity? Something else?
- What was an "enemy" your earliest family fought? (If your last name isn't Hatfield or McCoy, this might be a mind-bender. Be creative. Was it poverty? Class stigma? Something else?)
- What enemy is your family fighting today? (Again, be creative. There might be more than one answer.)

- **FOR YOUNGER TEAM MEMBERS:** In the movie *The Incredibles*, the whole family wears super-suits and battles evil together! What superpower would you give to each person in your family?

Game Plan

Together, identify one enemy that your family wants to conquer. Maybe it's consumption. Maybe it's cultural messages about body image for women and girls. Maybe it's poverty. Name your family's shared enemy and agree to fight it together.

NOTES

WEEK 31

Big Idea: The enemy your team is battling together might be small.

Teams can't live without mission and shared enemies. "Uh, Jefferson," you might protest, "I'm pretty sure what you're describing is called 'war,' not 'family.'" That's fair, and I hear you. To be clear, an enemy doesn't always prowl around in the dark or carry a gun. In our family, the enemy we battled together when we began growing vegetables was the soil! Maybe your enemy is the litter accumulating in your neighborhood or city. Maybe it's climate change. (Okay, that's a big one.) But it might be as simple as the scarcity of art supplies at a local grade school. Fight together; fight big; fight small.

- Last week, if you thought of a family that faced a big enemy, can you think of a family this week who is facing a smaller enemy?

- Did your earliest family unite to fight any shared battles? What were they, and how did that draw you closer?
- What are the enemies, or enemy, that your current family has battled together? (Even a one-day immersion experience counts.) What did the battle do for your team?
- **FOR YOUNGER TEAM MEMBERS:** Is there an obstacle or challenge people in your community are facing? Together, how can your family help?

Game Plan

If your family team hasn't identified a common enemy that needs to be thwarted, take some time this week to discuss it. What is each family team member passionate about? What lights their fire? What needs to be fixed?

NOTES

WEEK 32

Big Idea: Facing difficulty together can strengthen family teams.

A few years ago, when a business relationship and deep friendship went south, I was devastated. The emotional, financial, and spiritual consequences made me feel like I was being crushed 24-7. But I also grew some fruit during that season, which I never would have expected. Specifically, it was a season in our marriage in which Alyssa and I were deeply connected. I leaned on her for strength, wisdom, and encouragement in a way I'd never done before. Even our young children reached out to me with hugs, prayers, and gentle words. What the enemy meant for harm was transformed for our good. While I'd never wish that heartache on anyone, I became convinced that the difficulties we face together strengthen our family teams.

- Sometimes facing difficulty can weaken a family, but it can also strengthen it. What family have you seen strengthened by adversity?

- Have you weathered a difficult season in your earliest or current family? How?
- Have you known the kind of strengthening I experienced when facing a challenge together that you never would have chosen?
- **FOR YOUNGER TEAM MEMBERS:** When was the last time you helped a parent, sibling, or other family member? How did you help?

Game Plan

For this week's game plan, I'm not going to suggest looking for ways to be ripped off or forsaken by a loved one. Rather, have a family discussion about the hard times you have faced or might face, and commit to being a team that supports one another and grows from adversity.

NOTES

DIG DEEPER . . .

When we're a part of a family team, we don't face life's challenges alone: *We weather them together.*

And yet between doing laundry, driving to soccer practices, finishing homework, and preparing healthy meals, we may need a reminder to pause and notice the challenges we face.

This week, take time to notice the difficulties that each family member has faced over the last twelve months. With care and compassion, ask each family member to consider what he or she may have weathered over the last year, helping younger children to think about various areas of their lives.

- ○ Physical injury or illness
- ○ Educational challenges
- ○ Emotional difficulty, such as anxiety or depression
- ○ Relational challenges in the family
- ○ Relational challenges with friends
- ○ Spiritual challenges
- ○ Financial stress
- ○ Employment-related stress
- ○ Grief over death or other losses
- ○ Struggles with substance abuse
- ○ Lack of physical safety
- ○ Witness to harm or violence

After gently assessing each individual, pray for him or her, offering each concern to God.

WEEK 33

Big Idea: Children of all ages were designed to be more attached to family than to peers.

In middle school and high school, when many young people start pulling away from family and gravitating toward peers, parents tend to shrug their shoulders and accept their children's departure. Resigned, they simply observe, "Well, I guess this is happening now." And I get it. The force is strong. But this phenomena is relatively *new* in human history! I don't mean it's new in the last century; it's new in the history of human beings. So let's not accept it as a given condition and certainly not as a "good" one. Coaches, expect your players to stay on the team, and give them good reasons to!

- In what family or families have you witnessed teens and young adults remaining attached to their families in a healthy way?
- Coach, when you were a teen, did you pull away from your family

team and move toward peers as your primary social attachments? Did you and your friends view parents as the "enemy"?

- What are your expectations for members of your family team (who aren't yet grown) today?
- **FOR YOUNGER TEAM MEMBERS:** Being physically attached to family members is a good thing! How do you like to "attach" to your parent or caregiver? Piggyback rides? Snuggling on the couch? Something else?

Game Plan

Clearly name attachment, particularly in the teen years, as something your family values. Then brainstorm together ways to implement this value. What is expected of your family's teens, and what is expected of the rest of the team to make it work?

NOTES

WEEK 34

Big Idea: Gathering rituals offer "glue" that holds family teams together.

The most surprising thing I learned from Maté and Neufeld's research on adolescents was about "attachment affairs": how today's teenagers tend to detach from their families in favor of their peers. The researchers also explain what can prevent such detachment. They define "gathering" as a two-second eye-to-eye moment shared between parents and children when leaving one another and when returning. When you drop your child off at school, take two seconds (literally) to lock eyes. Then do the same when you reunite. Imagine the message you're sending is, "We are a team. I love you. We are in this together." That is what you want to communicate to your child, and that message holds teams together.

- Have you ever seen a family with a particular greeting or gathering ritual that bound them together in a unique way?

- When you were growing up, did someone communicate with their eyes that they were glad to see you? Share about that person.
- In the current rhythm and pace of your family's life together, are you pausing to communicate what matters most?
- **FOR YOUNGER TEAM MEMBERS:** Do your parents have a nickname for you that makes you feel special? Is there something, at bedtime or other times, you like to hear your parent say to you? What words of love, affirmation, or blessing do you like to hear?

Game Plan

Now is the time for your coaching staff to commit to creating moments of gathering (eye contact) with your players. You don't have to announce that you're starting this ritual. Just begin to capture moments to communicate to each family member that he or she is deeply valued.

NOTES

WEEK 35

Big Idea: Create a family mission statement.

Create a family mission statement. There. I said it. Because I'm more of a "How do we make an impact today?" kind of person, I resisted creating a family mission statement for years. I'd seen these cute decorative announcements in other homes, and they always felt more superficial than substantial. But I began to realize that it's not peripheral but *vital.* Businesses and athletic teams know this! The shared mission of any team filters and drives every small or large decision the team makes. Truly, it's magical. Creating a mission statement has the power to unlock team members' energy, focus, and potential. And I'll testify: our family's mission statement has guided us and helped us live out who we say we are.

- Do you know of a family, other than mine, who has implemented a mission statement? What is it?
- If your first family implemented a mission statement, how did it impact your shared sense of purpose?

- As you think about the possibility today, what would you say is the reason you do or do not currently have a family mission statement?
- **FOR YOUNGER TEAM MEMBERS:** How would you complete this sentence? "Our family should be ______________ together to bless the people and world God loves."

Game Plan

Take time with your team to noodle on your shared sense of mission and purpose. Don't rush. Begin to name your values and priorities. We created both a mission statement and also eight guiding pillars/values. (It took us three years!) Gather your ideas, let them marinate, and then clarify your shared purpose by writing a mission statement.

NOTES

WEEK 36

Big Idea: Distinguish between *mission* and *assignment.*

It's important to note and honor the difference between *mission* and *assignment. Mission* is about the overarching purpose that guides your family. You might have a sense that it's "hospitality" or "bridging generations" or something else. But *assignment* is the vehicle through which you live out your mission. So if your mission is to offer mercy and compassion to those on the world's margins, your assignment might be working with folks from your church to feed the hungry. Or it might be standing outside the local prison on Christmas morning and singing songs of hope. Or befriending a family that includes a child with Down syndrome and inviting that child to your kids' parties. Your family's shared mission is what guides you to identify assignments that have your family's name on them.

- You've considered families that share a mission. Can you think of a particular assignment that you've seen carried out by a family you know?

- As you clarify the mission and assignments for your family, you might also do the same for yourself. Over the years, has a particular mission—named or unnamed—guided you to say yes to various assignments?
- As a family, notice the kinds of assignments to which you're already saying yes. Is there a common theme among them?
- **FOR YOUNGER TEAM MEMBERS:** When was the last time your family worked together to help others? What did you do?

Game Plan

Distinguishing between *mission* and *assignment* this week is a great opportunity for your crew to notice whether you've been faithful to accept assignments! What assignments have you completed in the past twelve months, and which ones might have your name on them in the next year?

NOTES

WEEK 37

Big Idea: Identifying particular seasons can nourish and sustain your team.

If a ball team had to train year after year without playing a game, or if they played back-to-back games for years on end, they'd likely find the rhythm to be unsustainable. Teams know what each season is for: training, competing, rest, etc. Alyssa and I have found a lot of traction by naming the three-month seasons we notice unfolding for our team. One quarter might be a "put our heads down and work hard" season. Another might be a "rest up and recharge" season. Or another might be a "learn a new skill and grow together" season. Notice that each season serves our team's common mission, allowing us to be the best team we can be.

- In earlier generations of your family, can you recognize seasons you may have experienced together? What would you name those seasons?

- When you don't note and name your team's current season, you may find an imbalance in the ratio of conditioning to competing, preparing for, and executing your mission. Have you noticed this imbalance at all in your family team?
- What type of season is your family in today?
- **FOR YOUNGER TEAM MEMBERS:** For the world to be fruitful, each year is broken up into four seasons: winter, spring, summer, and fall. What's your favorite? Why?

Game Plan

This week, develop a mechanism by which you can huddle up and notice the season your family is experiencing. Maybe you set a three-month alarm on the coaches' calendars. Or maybe write your season's name on the family calendar. Identify a practical way to identify new seasons of your family's life.

NOTES

WEEK 38

Big Idea: Your family was designed to be a family *on* mission.

As we look at various types of missional families, we'll notice that while some may have had the best of intentions, their particular execution was lacking. What I'm calling "Family *and* Mission" puts family in one bucket and mission in another. The designated missionary has to leave the family to accomplish the mission. And we can also notice "Family *as* Mission" families: when families make *themselves* the mission. The insular path of producing a nice, perfect, moral family fails to usher in God's will on earth as it is in heaven. And that's why I believe "Family *on* Mission" to be the better goal. A family on mission moves out into the world to build God's kingdom on earth together. Collectively they accomplish what they can't accomplish alone.

- As you consider the intentionally missional families you've known, can you (kindly, gently) identify all three types?

- What kind of a pivot might make these families even more effective as agents of God's kingdom?
- Today, which of the three types of missional families most accurately describes your own? Say why.
- **FOR YOUNGER TEAM MEMBERS:** Can you think of something that your family has done together that one person couldn't have done alone? (If this is hard, ask a parent for help.)

Game Plan

Remember how mission statements are supposed to be more than a cute wall decoration? They're *actionable*. So as you consider becoming a family on mission, what slight pivot could help your family be more effective at living out your mission?

NOTES

DIG DEEPER . . .

For a long time I resisted creating a family mission statement. Eventually, though, I realized it was vital. If we don't know why we exist or where we're going, how will we ever get there? Today I am such a big fan of our family mission statement because when we've needed it most, it's given us direction, helped us make decisions, and reminded every team member what we're about. Here is our mission statement:

> We exist primarily to fulfill Jesus' words by living out "Your kingdom come, your will be done, on Maui, as it is in heaven" in our family, neighborhood, relationships, vocation, and all that we do.
>
> The eight pillars that guide us in fulfilling this mission are:
>
> 1. We are apprentices to Jesus.
> 2. Family is a team sport.
> 3. We center the table in everything.
> 4. Nothing is ours. We are generous.
> 5. Create more than we consume.
> 6. Live rhythmically.
> 7. Live multigenerationally.
> 8. Practice holistic health.

Please read through your mission statement (from week 35) and discuss whether or not it adequately captures your "family on mission" goal. This would be a great time to add pillars to your mission. While you're free to borrow appropriate parts of our statement and pillars, you'll be more successful if you spend time over the next few weeks and months discussing who *your* family is and what you're about. It might help to create a list of values first, and then revise your mission statement based on those.

Don't rush this. Let it bake.

When you've completed the revision of your family's mission statement, share it with another family you love and trust. And find creative ways to keep it in front of your family members!

WEEK 39

Big Idea: We can be tempted to sacrifice our families on the altar of money.

When religious folks quote 1 Timothy 6:10, "For the love of money is a root of all kinds of evil," it's easy enough to conjure an image of someone like Disney's Cruella de Vil or Scrooge McDuck—caricatures who have been completely corrupted by greed. And, to be fair, that kind of addiction is harmful. But let's dial it back to where we live: where we hustle at work to pay back school debt, pay the mortgage, buy new cars and the newest gaming systems, and still have money left over to take summer and winter vacations. That's pretty normal, isn't it? Yet when we give ourselves over to work to pay for more stuff, we risk sacrificing our families. So I want to say it clearly: Your kids don't need a certain lifestyle. They need *you*.

- Can you think of a family on television or in the movies that sacrificed itself at the altar of "money"? What did that look like?

- In the family in which you were raised, did you ever feel like your designated caregivers prioritized work outside the home above family? If so, did you ever express that feeling?
- Today, do you see yourself as someone who hustles at work but is absent at home?
- **FOR YOUNGER TEAM MEMBERS:** Isn't it awesome being with your mom or your dad? What is your favorite thing to do with your mom? Your dad?

Game Plan

I'm not throwing shade on breadwinners. The bread has to be won. This week, have a discussion about what your family needs and what your family wants. Look for creative ways to ensure your family's needs are met, and make choices that prioritize meaningful time together—in both quality and quantity!

NOTES

WEEK 40

Big Idea: We can be tempted to sacrifice our families on the altar of purpose.

As noble as it may sound, we can be tempted to sacrifice our families in the name of "purpose." And when I am naming this particular temptation—and even "holy purpose," I'll add!—I am keenly aware that this is where I live. What I mean is, because of the work I do, it would be really easy to be seduced by some sense of personal higher purpose. So let me make it plain: Once you're part of a family team, "mission" is no longer solitary. Even when you leave home for an assignment, you're being sent by the home team as their ambassador to accomplish the team's mission in the world.

- Can you think of a family you've known or heard of that has been sacrificed on the altar of purpose?
- Where have you noticed individuals around you, even ones you

respect, making the decision to sacrifice family in the name of purpose? (Even a good purpose!)

- How is your family balancing this today?
- **FOR YOUNGER TEAM MEMBERS:** Was there ever a time when your parent was away doing a "good thing"—doing their job or even helping others—when you missed them and wished they were at home? Talk about that time.

Game Plan

Some churches announce their purpose during worship service *every single Sunday*. Every member of those churches is clear about the body's single driving purpose. And it doesn't hurt to repeat your family's own purpose frequently either. This week, remind one another of the team's purpose and notice whether you are balancing the team's purpose with the team's togetherness.

NOTES

WEEK 41

Big Idea: When only one person is winning, the whole team is losing.

Can we just address the way that so many mothers are being pulled tug-of-war-style today? Plenty of evangelical churches want to see moms at home raising children alone, à la the 1950s family experiment, while dad is out getting his purpose on. Other voices in the culture want women to receive and take advantage of the kinds of work opportunities men have traditionally had. Neither one of those are inherently bad tracks for women, but we do need to be honest about how our choices strain the family team. Whether moms at home are denied opportunities to flourish or whether they're submitted to the tyranny of work men have typically known, the team loses. When a family is healthy and balanced and unified, the whole team wins.

- Do you know of a family in which one person's win led to another's loss?

- As you think about your earliest home, can you identify one person who was "winning," or experiencing fulfillment, at the expense of others?
- Today, how would you evaluate the balance or imbalance—in terms of flourishing and fulfillment—on your team?
- **FOR YOUNGER TEAM MEMBERS:** What's one game or activity you play where only one person can win? Can you think of a game or activity where *everyone* can win?

Game Plan

If you identify one person on your team who is flourishing at the expense of others, look for one practical change you could make this week to regain balance. It's possible that this conversation can happen without the little ones being present—though you might be surprised by their contributions!

NOTES

WEEK 42

Big Idea: Effective teams deploy all their assets.

Okay, this week is a fun one. I want to suggest that you might have secret assets on your team that are just waiting to be put into operation. Maybe you have leadership skills that no one else in the family does. Or maybe your spouse has operational gifts or visioning capabilities that no one else has. Maybe your oldest child is particularly sensitive to people's difficulties and knows how to comfort them. Or perhaps another has a brilliant mind for problem solving. I think you can see where this is going! Your team is going to be strengthened when you identify and deploy the many assets at your disposal.

- What family do you know that has done a great job of deploying all of their members to do what only they can do?
- Before engaging deeply, are you aware right now of assets on your team that aren't being utilized?
- What key assets are being utilized by each member on your team today?

- **FOR YOUNGER TEAM MEMBERS:** Name one special skill or gift or talent or asset that each family member shares with the whole family.

Game Plan

If you've already done a team scouting report, this is the moment to pull it out! If you haven't yet done one, now is the time. Review or identify the strengths and gifts of each team member and name concrete ways that each team member is contributing or *can be* contributing his or her assets.

NOTES

WEEK 43

Big Idea: Effective family teams are integrated across various ages.

If you look around the community where you live, you're going to notice the ways that we naturally—or unnaturally!—segregate people by age. Perhaps we assume disintegration is the best model, so we don't ask any questions. We assume classrooms need to be segregated by age, even though rural one-room schoolhouses have worked in the past. We assume Sunday school classes need to be segregated by age, even though some of the most innovative churches are working to reintegrate Christian education. Or we might assume that because our community has a senior center, "they have their place." But guess what? "Their place" comes alive when children show up. In the same way, families that are intentional about reintegrating—running errands together, sharing work trips, or taking special adventures—are stronger for it.

- What robust family have you known that was successfully integrated across a variety of ages?
- As you think about your own childhood, in what spaces did you experience segregation by age?
- Today, where do you see creative solutions to the separation of individuals by age?
- **FOR YOUNGER TEAM MEMBERS:** Something special happens when kids and old folks get together. Who is an older adult with whom you get to spend time? And what is your favorite way to share time with that person?

Game Plan

As a family, discuss where your family is experiencing disintegration. Does mom travel frequently for work? Does a teen spend thirty hours a week outside the home with his girlfriend? Notice your weak spots and brainstorm creative solutions to reintegrate your squad.

NOTES

WEEK 44

Big Idea: Share ownership of the family with children.

Do you want your six-year-old choosing every item that goes into the grocery cart? Not likely. Or should you put your fifteen-year-old in charge of the family finances? At your own peril. But while I'm clear that coaches need to be *leading* the team, there are all kinds of ways to give children a voice within the family. For example, when I get invitations to speak far from home, Alyssa and the kids weigh in. Or maybe you have been offered a leadership role at your church, but you welcome all members of the family to offer their thoughts before you accept or reject the opportunity. In a culture where relocating is often largely determined by "dad's job," invite all your team members to discuss the prospect of moving. Show every member of the team that his or her voice matters.

- When have you witnessed parents doing a great job of sharing ownership of the family with children? What, specifically, did that look like?

- When you were growing up, did you have a sense of participating in family decisions? Share more.
- As you examine your team today, do you notice some members whose voices need to be amplified? Muted? (LOL—no muting! Maybe dialed down?)
- **FOR YOUNGER TEAM MEMBERS:** Have you ever had a vote about what job an adult in your family took? How about where your family lived, where you went on vacation, or what you all did for fun on the weekend? (What *would* you like to have a say in?)

Game Plan

Have a coaches meeting this week—or meet with yourself!—to identify some forthcoming family decisions in which you could welcome team input. Determine those areas where children's voices, in particular, might be really useful. Be creative!

NOTES

DIG DEEPER . . .

You may agree with the idea that every family member's voice matters, but in order to live it out, you have to make it practical.

Schedule a family listening session this week so the voices and opinions of all your team members can be heard. As you review the regular rhythms of your household, ask two questions:

1. On a scale of 1–10, how life-giving would you score our rhythms right now?
2. Do we need to improve our current practices? How?

Here are some areas to discuss, and you may identify others:

- ☐ Meals and nutrition
- ☐ Bedtimes and rest
- ☐ Exercise, physical activity
- ☐ Chores, indoor
- ☐ Chores, outdoor
- ☐ Pet care
- ☐ Money
- ☐ Consumption of *stuff*
- ☐ Hospitality
- ☐ Giving and stewardship

- ☐ Vacation, travel
- ☐ Worship
- ☐ Sabbath
- ☐ Prayer

You may expect to hear suggestions like "no bedtimes," "no chores," and "pizza for every meal." It's okay to make room for these suggestions, but it's also fair to filter them. These questions can help you decide which suggestions/changes are worth considering:

- Is it safe?
- Is it healthy?
- Is it for our good?
- Is it good for others?

Keep an open mind as you listen, and you might be surprised at what you hear!

After this process, decide together which areas you'll choose to recalibrate.

WEEK 45

Big Idea: A win for families is expecting "high demand" and offering "high support."

I was blown away when our acquaintance Sarah described how her employers set her free—after just two weeks on the job—to purchase a *warehouse*. (Yeah, not *housewares* but *warehouse*.) Her bosses communicated to her exactly what Alyssa and I want to communicate to our children: "We believe in you. We trust you. We know you can do this." And when I saw it in action with my own eyes, I realized that the win for organizations is the same win for families: Expect "high demand" and offer "high support." We're like the teacher who tells her student, "I have very high expectations of you, and I know you can reach them." Then we offer the child the support he or she needs to succeed.

- Can you think of a family you know that has expected a lot from its members and also supported them well?
- As you think about these two variables, *demand* and *support*,

how did they affect your experience in your earliest family? Did you experience high demand? Low demand? High support? Low support?

- At this moment, how would you say your family is operating in terms of expectations and support?
- **FOR YOUNGER TEAM MEMBERS:** Has your parent ever let you do something you weren't sure you could do? What was it? (Walk a neighbor's dog? Rake the lawn? Something else?) How did your mom or dad help you succeed?

Game Plan

While this big idea is indeed transformational, you need to be intentional about execution. As a coach, notice the areas where you can expect more of your team members and then brainstorm how you can offer them the support they need to succeed.

NOTES

WEEK 46

Big Idea: Your words can shape the vision a team member has of himself or herself.

One conversation with my middle school principal changed the way I saw myself. (And, yeah, I was in his office because I was being kicked out of school for my behavior.) Comparing me to an unfinished sculpture, he suggested that a master hand was shaping me into something worthwhile, but that I wasn't quite finished yet. He offered, "I see an incredibly talented and bright and kind young man in there who will come out if you keep working at it." Did I still struggle? I did. But the seed that was planted that day began to grow. And when others watered it, it continued to grow.

- Sometimes we'll overhear a parent saying something powerful to a member of their family team. What life-giving words have you heard shared in other families?

- Has anyone in your life, like Principal Adleman, seen more in you than you saw in yourself?
- Today, are you embracing this practice of letting your children know the good that you see in them?
- **FOR YOUNGER TEAM MEMBERS:** What adult has told you they saw something good in you? And what did he or she say to you? ("You have creative gifts." "You're great at finding things." "You are a great leader." "I like the way you care for your sister." "You did a great job solving that problem.")

Game Plan

This doesn't need to be particularly orderly or systematic, but make a goal of pausing to have a moment with each of your children when you reflect for them the good, the potential, and the promise you see in them. Eyeball-to-eyeball, give them a glimpse of who you see them becoming.

NOTES

WEEK 47

Big Idea: Effective family teams shift their language from *me* to *we*.

While I was single, I naturally thought in terms of *me* and not *we*. Of course. And when I got married I had to learn to shift, as anyone does, to thinking as *we* and not *me*. At the insistence of an older brother, I also decided to change my language—*we* changed *our* language—to *we*. At first I was unconvinced that a little mind game like *changing one letter in a word* could help shift my whole perspective. I mean, that's crazy, right? But it did help. So no longer was *I* leaving home to speak at a conference; *we* were sending an ambassador of Team Bethke to do the work we shared. And if you give this a whirl, you'll likely also notice that once you start *speaking* it, you will become better at *living* it!

- Can you think of a family you've encountered who uses *we* more than they use *me*? What do you notice about the posture that family's members have toward one another?

- As you think back to your first home, do you remember more *we* conversations or more *me* conversations?
- On a scale of 1–10 (1 being *me* and 10 being *we*), where would you say your family team is today in terms of thinking corporately rather than individually?
- **FOR YOUNGER TEAM MEMBERS:** You might say of yourself: "I'm a good speller." "I'm a good artist." "I'm a helper." Thinking about your family and its strengths, how would you finish this sentence: "*We* are ____________"?

Game Plan

Invite all the members of your team to try an experiment. For one week, try not to use *me* or *I* and instead try to speak using *we*. (I recognize the obvious perils and impracticalities, but you'll still discover something from trying.) Help one another with reminders, and then discuss the experiment at the end of the week.

NOTES

WEEK 48

Big Idea: A regular rhythm of rest blesses families.

The eleven-year experiment of a seven-day workweek in the Soviet Union was a big fail. Rather than productivity rising—by keeping humans and machines in constant motion—it actually fell. Families were disrupted. Even the machines could not keep up! And while a seven-day week seems, in some ways, arbitrary, across times and cultures it has proven most effective. Researchers have called the rhythm of six work days and then one for rest a "tool" of rest and repair. And I'm convinced that this tool is one that serves and blesses our families. In fact, when families intent on building a family team ask where to start, the answer is always *Sabbath*. Families who craft a day of rest are refreshed and ready for the work God has called them to do.

- Have you witnessed another family integrating *rest* into their Sabbath?
- How is your family currently practicing Sabbath?
- What's working well, and what could be improved?

- **FOR YOUNGER TEAM MEMBERS:** In the past, when your family has paused to take a day off and spend time together, what family activities have you most enjoyed?

Game Plan

Gather your family team and talk about "rest." During the week, how much physical rest does each member need at night? And on the Sabbath, what does and does not feel restful for each member? In what creative way can your family claim rest on the Sabbath you share?

NOTES

WEEK 49

Big Idea: A family Sabbath becomes the high point of the week.

For those who find identity in their work, the idea of Sabbath might feel like a real bummer. And for those who use the constant buzz of work to soothe the constant buzz inside, the possibility of *stopping* might even feel a little scary. But I'm not talking about creating a day where everything stops; I'm inviting you to create a day where everything shifts. To be clear, a family Sabbath isn't something to dread. If you do it right—if you liberate members from the workweek, create a relational atmosphere, and eat ice cream together while you watch movies—the Sabbath can become the high point of your family's week.

- Have you ever noticed a family who shared a healthy Sabbath? How did they do it? What practices did they adopt?
- As you think back to your first family, what did Sabbath look

like? Was it a day you eagerly anticipated or one you dreaded? Why?

- Did you learn anything new or inspiring about family Sabbath that feels like it would be a good fit for your family team?
- **FOR YOUNGER TEAM MEMBERS:** If you had a whole day to enjoy with your family—no phones, no computers, no interruptions—how would you spend it?

Game Plan

As you consider taking a break from the regular work of the week, what practices does your family want to begin to implement today? Discuss what a Sabbath "win" will look like for your family team. When you reach agreement, remind yourself of shared expectations by posting them on the fridge.

NOTES

WEEK 50

Big Idea: Have the courage to say "no" on the Sabbath.

For people pleasers, one of the scariest words in the English language is *no*. If you have healthy boundaries, you might not find it frightening at all. But for those who've built their identity on saying yes to every opportunity, *no* might feel foreign. But it is *faithful*. In order to say yes to Sabbath, it's necessary to say no to other things. Maybe it means saying no to small-screen (like iPad small) individual entertainment. Maybe it means that no one goes to the grocery store or Target on the Sabbath because there are six other days for those grueling jobs. Or maybe you gather the courage to say no to youth sports on Sundays. Or you might simply say no to kids visiting friends' homes but say yes to friends joining your family for Sabbath rest and togetherness. Having the courage to say no is what protects a Sabbath that will bless your family.

- Have you seen other families set boundaries around their Sabbath day by saying no to other things? What did they reject?

- As you think about the kind of nos that will ultimately bless your team members, which are the easiest?
- And which are the most difficult nos your family needs to say?
- **FOR YOUNGER TEAM MEMBERS:** If you could invite one friend to spend special time with your family on the Sabbath, who would you want to invite?

Game Plan

As you create a Sabbath that will best serve your family team, decide together what you are saying no to. And then discuss and decide what you are saying yes to.

NOTES

DIG DEEPER . . .

Our family and others have found such peace and joy by committing to a day of shared Sabbath with one another. It isn't a day we dread; it's a day we look forward to enjoying.

If you haven't yet been intentional about creating a protected Sabbath day for your family, now is your chance. I'm going to suggest you begin by choosing that to which you are saying yes, and then protect your yeses by naming what you plan to say no to.

WE SAY YES TO:

- ☐ Play
- ☐ Sharing a good meal
- ☐ Rest
- ☐ Recreation, games, sports
- ☐ Laughter, joy, humor
- ☐ Pleasure and delight
- ☐ Celebration
- ☐ Spending time outdoors
- ☐ Dessert
- ☐ Food
- ☐ More food
- ☐ Sharing entertainment
- ☐ Hospitality
- ☐ Candle lighting

- ☐ Caring for one another
- ☐ One-on-one time among family members
- ☐ Creating
- ☐ Doing what our members love to do
- ☐ Blessing one another
- ☐ Blessing others
- ☐ Sharing stories
- ☐ Other __________

WE SAY NO TO:

- ☐ Stress
- ☐ Busyness
- ☐ Entertainment that separates us rather than draws us closer
- ☐ Our phones, social media, work email
- ☐ Work that pays the bills
- ☐ Shopping
- ☐ Kids' and parents' commitments, teams, and activities outside the home
- ☐ Other __________

Consider posting your family's Sabbath commitments inside the door of your kitchen cabinet for easy reference!

WEEK 51

Big Idea: Enjoy family trips to celebrate, not sustain.

If you have a job outside of the home and are burning the candle at both ends by working long hours, a weeklong vacation at the beach with your family won't *fix* the damage caused by the fifty-one weeks you missed. Or if you're *all* so overprogrammed and overworked that you begin counting down the days until vacation ninety days out, you likely need more than a week at the beach! Using vacation to save the family isn't the goal. Family trips are meant to be a special time for celebrating and enjoying one another—not a time for "fixing" the family.

- Have you witnessed another family taking a particularly unique or interesting family trip together? What about their adventure or celebration appealed to you?
- In your first family, what types of trips or vacations did you take together? What was the best thing about them? What felt like the hardest thing about them?
- In your current family, what types of trips have you shared? Is

there anything that needs to be adjusted in the way you get away together?

- **FOR YOUNGER TEAM MEMBERS:** When you think about trips your family has taken, what is your favorite memory?

Game Plan

Discuss the trips you've taken as a family, describing the highlights for everyone and what might have been more difficult moments. What unique family celebration or traditions would you like to include in your family trips?

NOTES

WEEK 52

Big Idea: Practice giving as a team.

From their earliest days, our children learn from culture to become consumers. A toy in a cereal box markets the newest family movie. The movie spawns action figures, T-shirts, and pajamas featuring the movie's hero. But what's *one* superhero action figure without the rest of the good guys, the bad guys, and all the vehicles they drive? However, you can flip the script of consumerism that's been handed to you by becoming a family that contributes rather than consumes. Maybe you have a special account, like we do, that can be used for giving. Or maybe each child can choose whether a portion of their allowance will be shared to help others. It's important for your children to see you giving and to see the impact it has on the lives of the people God loves.

- Although giving is often private, sometimes we get a glimpse of how other families give. What family have you seen being generous? How?
- In your first family, was *giving* a priority? When did you see your

family contributing to meet the needs of others, either people you knew personally or those farther away?

- Does your family team have a mechanism in place for contributing to the needs of others? Is it transparent, so that all the members of the family team have a sense of ownership and participation?
- **FOR YOUNGER TEAM MEMBERS:** If each member of your family put some money in a jar to give away, how would *you* choose to spend that money? What person or work would you want to support?

Game Plan

Even if you've been giving as a family, pause this week to discuss why you give and how you give. Because a monthly bank draft or credit card statement is hard for younger children to conceptualize, consider how they can participate in giving: for example, writing to a child you sponsor overseas, baking a meal to share with an elderly neighbor, or helping to serve meals at a shelter.

NOTES

Family Summit

FAMILY MISSION STATEMENT:

CORE FAMILY VALUES/PILLARS:

REVIEW OF LAST YEAR—BIG PICTURE QUESTIONS:

1. How and when did we live up to our mission statement?

2. Which core values did we achieve?

3. Which value was the strongest?

STORY OF THE YEAR

If you were to retell the story of the year in five minutes, what would you say? Each of you pretend you are talking to a friend whom you haven't seen in the last year. You're holding your coffees, and your friend says, "Catch me up on how you've been. What has God been doing in your life, and what have you been up to?"

IMPORTANT: Do this exercise separately first, then come together to share. After you've all shared, ask these questions:

1. What did your family members include that you didn't?

2. Whose story felt happier than the others?

3. What had you forgotten that another family member reminded you of?

4. Was your story of the last year one you were pleased or proud to tell? Why or why not?

LOSSES FROM LAST YEAR

Write down a few of the losses your family experienced during the last year. Reminder: Losses can be any area in which you've grieved, any area that seemed difficult for a long season, anything you miss that hasn't come back, and so on. Mark an *X* next to any losses that still feel like a loss, and mark with a + any losses that were hard but that—through new perspective—have begun to feel like redemption. This is basically a section to talk about the hard things in a free-flowing way. Adjust the questions to your children's capacity. You may want to keep some of the following discussions between parents.

Questions to ask each team member:

1. What would you say was the hardest moment of this year? Why?
2. What did you learn from the losses, or did the losses change you in any way?
3. Where did you see God showing up the most this year?
4. Look for patterns. Was God teaching you or nudging you toward a particular theme of growth?
5. What is one area in which you saw the most growth and that you are proud of?
6. What is something new you did or implemented that seemed to work? What is something you are glad you did? (Examples: date night once a month, no phones in bedrooms, etc.)
7. Where did God surprise you?
8. What did you do this year that will benefit you fifty years from now?

WINS FROM LAST YEAR

Write down the wins, both small and big.

Questions to ask each team member:

1. What would you say is the biggest win from this past year?

2. What's one thing that was hard but that ended well? Are you glad or thankful for that hard thing?
3. What are five things you are thankful for this year?
4. What's something that happened this year that you never would've expected?
5. What was your favorite date as a married couple this year?
6. What is the best memory you made this year as a couple?

FINANCES

1. What is the worst financial decision we made this year? Why?
2. What's one way we can change how we see, spend, or use finances next year?
3. What was the best "fun" purchase we made this year?
4. What was our most memorable moment of generosity and stewardship this year?
5. How did God take care of us this year financially? How did he provide?

TRAVEL

1. At a glance: What travel do we have planned this coming year?
2. Which trip are we most excited about?
3. What do we hope for with the travel?
4. How can we set ourselves up for success in our travels?
5. Which trips will be family trips, dad-only trips, dad-with-a-kid trips, mom-only trips, mom-with-a-kid trips, etc.?

CHILDREN

1. Take a look back at your scouting report. What still rings true about our team?
2. How would you update your scouting report?
3. What is one word to describe how our parent/child relationships went this past year?
4. How are our kids excelling as individuals?
5. With what does each kid need some extra help?
6. How can we call out their true identity in the Lord more in the next year?
7. What was the best thing we instituted with the kids that blessed our family this year (new traditions, training tools, etc.)?

FAVORITES

FAVORITE	ANSWER
Memory	
Date	
Moment with kids	
Movie we watched	
Meal	
Moment with friends	
New thing we did	
Place of growth	
New habit	
Praise in our community	
Book	

RHYTHM AND FORMATION DIAGNOSTIC

Remember: rhythms are not routines. Routines are what you do to make sure life goes on as needed (tie your shoes every morning, go to work, etc.). But rhythms are voluntary choices we make throughout the day and week and year to fill our days and moments with life-giving activities. Another way to put it is, rhythms are the formational choices we make every day to be a certain type of person or family. Repetitive practices that turn our hearts and minds toward the "north star" of the family we want to be. And that can be something fun, serious, long, short, and so on! But easily one of the best ways to grow at rhythms is to make sure you are consistently taking stock of how it's going and how they are doing—rhythms are meant to be tweaked and adapted and evolve for years and years as we slowly refine them into better and better practices!

What daily, weekly, and yearly rhythms are shaping your family?

Daily rhythms include starting the day with a mantra or question, sharing a thankful list at the dinner table, or praying before bedtime. Weekly rhythms might mean sharing a special family meal on the Sabbath or finding other ways to make the Sabbath a day of rest and delight. Or various family members might establish weekly rhythms that include sibling one-on-ones, date nights, or business meetings. Your family might also choose to embrace yearly rhythms. This Family Summit is one of them. But you might also consider marking meaningful anniversaries or biblical holidays with a big party. Take note of the ways your family is currently embracing life-giving rhythms together.

DAILY	WEEKLY	YEARLY

Rhythm Reflection

1. Which rhythm gave us the most life this year? Which rhythm could we not have lived without?
2. Which rhythm needs more work or tweaking to inspire optimal results?
3. Are there new rhythms we want to add?
4. Any rhythms we want to change?
5. Any rhythms we want to take away?

FOR MARRIAGE PARTNERS

Sin and Battle

1. Where do you feel like sin patterns most entered into our marriage or our individual lives this year?
2. How do you think your sin affected our marriage and family?
3. What did God reveal to you about yourself this year, or how did he help you resist temptation, the devil, the flesh, and the world?

4. What is the most helpful thing I do as a spouse when your sin patterns begin to show?
5. What is the least helpful thing I do as a spouse when it comes to those areas?
6. Where did you see God triumph over sin in your life, marriage, and family this year? Be specific. Count the blessings and moments of victory. What about in areas of weakness, hurt, pain, or any type of serious spiritual battle that doesn't include sin?

Thankfulness Section

List twenty things you are thankful for this past year. Big or small. Fun or serious.

1. ______________________________
2. ______________________________
3. ______________________________
4. ______________________________
5. ______________________________
6. ______________________________
7. ______________________________
8. ______________________________
9. ______________________________
10. ______________________________
11. ______________________________
12. ______________________________
13. ______________________________
14. ______________________________
15. ______________________________

16. ______________________________
17. ______________________________
18. ______________________________
19. ______________________________
20. ______________________________

Ceremony and Altar

Build some type of altar or curate some type of moment to close this activity and year. Moments and seasons have to be marked. Do something that breaks the script from your normal day or routine. Go to a nice restaurant to celebrate God's faithfulness; craft something that represents what you talk about and hang it up on the fridge as a reminder throughout the year; or plant a flower or tree in the backyard to represent the past year and God's goodness and blessing.

1. How will we choose to mark this year?
2. How will we choose to remember this year?
3. Fifty years from now, what do we want our kids to remember about this year? How can we commemorate for them the blessings of this year?

Notes

1. D'Vera Cohn and Jeffrey S. Passel, "A Record 64 Million Americans Live in Multigenerational Households," Pew Research Center, April 5, 2018, https://www.pewresearch.org/fact-tank/2018/04/05/a-record-64-million-americans-live-in-multigenerational-households.
2. Bill and Melinda Gates, "Why Giving Away Our Wealth Has Been the Most Satisfying Thing We've Done," TED.com, March 2014, https://www.ted.com/talks/bill_and_melinda_gates_why_giving_away_our_wealth_has_been_the_most_satisfying_thing_we_ve_done/transcript?language=en.

About the Author

Jefferson Bethke is the *New York Times* bestselling author of *Jesus > Religion*, *It's Not What You Think*, *To Hell with the Hustle*, *Love That Lasts*, and *Take Back Your Family.* He and his wife, Alyssa, host *The Real Life Podcast* and run FamilyTeams.com, an online initiative equipping families to live as a multigenerational team on mission. They live in Maui with their daughters, Kinsley and Lucy, and son, Kannon. To say hi or to learn more, go to http://jeffandalyssa.com.